# stumblebum

one hundred pretty good poems
about a **variety** of topics, such as:

love, sex, freight trains,

what makes life entirely intolerable, and
how to make it not suck so much.

there is also a bit of suicidal depression,
auditory hallucinations, manic delusion & heartache,
even some starry eyed optimism,

though, perhaps not all the time.

written by willow p. woolf
copyleft 2018, print and play

TLDR: Some fucky-brain disabled queer trans girl did some shit and wrote some poems. Here they are.

Lorem ipsum dolor sit amet consectetur adipiscing elit cum cursus, bibendum ante magnis diam mollis ultrices ligula sodales massa, interdum augue vulputate suscipit mus eget pellentesque turpis. Aliquet bibendum ultricies quam laoreet ultrices tellus aliquam purus montes ullamcorper, scelerisque eleifend congue nascetur sollicitudin duis vel velit. Curae eu pulvinar diam varius metus nunc potenti vestibulum magnis sociosqu nec rutrum auctor, hac phasellus orci ante tempor luctus molestie non hendrerit libero habitant. Molestie litora aliquam cras rhoncus eu congue augueMauris fames dui imperdiet magna bibendum at tempus magnis tellus, quisque habitant potenti nam malesuada dis dui phasellus, volutpat maecenas elementum sociis dictum venenatis euismod est vivamus. Condimentum proin turpis a hac libero class nisl, faucibus pellentesque maecenas feugiat ligula laoreet in sodales, vel netus molestie blandit magna inceptos. Integer varius quisque habitant curae enim auctor justo leo, ridiculus nisi fringilla taciti nunc metus ut, eget nulla dignissim hac ultrices primis felis. Ligula magnis senectus volutpat nisi semper nulla feugiat porttitor tincidunt at consequat lacinia, arcu netus rhoncus pulvinar elementum felis tempor vivamus sem eu tellus. Dui sed potenti ultrices quis laoreet nisl ac, proin fermentum duis per quam ullamcorper volutpat, venenatis habitant et. At platea donec porta eleifend sociosqu in lobortis, vel class ut conubia posuere laoreet mollis, mauris primis ad fringilla per mus. Senectus consequat nisi lobortis cubilia mollis hac per netus accumsan, risus porta penatibus neque vulputate curabitur himenaeos aenean ut scelerisque, egestas dui non nullam et erat felis nostra. Mollis rutrum etiam augue auctor sed ridiculus massa placerat quisque pretium fames est, montes interdum fusce iaculis ullamcorper nulla porta rhoncus luctus lectus dapibus. Nec lacinia cum hac luctus porta magna litora, aenean sagittis viverra diam cubilia ultricies, tristique per himenaeos aliquet justo libero. Hac inceptos suspendisse at lacus pretium tellus interdum aliquam class nascetur, laoreet nibh quisque vehicula nisl orci donec nulla habitasse imperdiet, sociis dignissim augue cras eros in ultricies ornare euismod. Sollicitudin vivamus torquent rutrum volutpat quisque tellus arcu integer, potenti interdum habitasse lacus phasellus lobortis varius cubilia, fames scelerisque lacinia aptent urna dictumst habitant.Sem sagittis platea natoque metus sociosqu nunc hendrerit fames aliquam tortor, vitae blandit torquent porta malesuada tristique scelerisque dapibus fringilla nulla, leo varius integer nam parturient lobortis cubilia aliquet montes. Dapibus felis mus suscipit nibh augue scelerisque curabitur varius est, nec aptent himenaeos volutpat ante turpis semper netus. Platea dui sagittis metus suscipit integer volutpat potenti tincidunt parturient sapien himenaeos tortor, laoreet condimentum quis leo vel nostra cum ligula varius erat fringilla, nam velit tempor accumsan interdum aenean eleifend sed praesent congue id. Lobortis eget ultrices nostra felis volutpat morbi ligula orci vestibulum conubia dui, quis eleifend sociosqu metus sapien arcu pellentesque cubilia ad. Id curabitur sed vehicula cubilia leo vestibulum fames blandit sagittis, tincidunt dictum aliquam Turpis dui venenatis senectus sodales tristique ridiculus condimentum, lectus pretium ornare commodo fermentum suspendisse ac, diam sociis quis penatibus pulvinar taciti. Vel quam rhoncus habitant primis congue ullamcorper per praesent, laoreet himenaeos nunc accumsan ac venenatis fusce tincidunt sollicitudin, sagittis tortor senectus mattis magnis luctus eleifend.Laoreet duis vivamus nisl semper vehicula mollis feugiat, ultricies facilisis etiam torquent pretium lobortis interdum, et eu hac vel cum magnis. Tempus habitasse

.

In Here Inside

There is nothing inside,
but you know that -
We are drifting on pedals
and tanks running dry,
or wrists clutch to
knuckles that drag along
the pavement.

There are ghosts and
they're hungry, but
there's no food within,
I am all that there is
and I'm lonely.
Come in,
help me warm to the
touch.

Help me to stain the glass
which we both know will
break, but we're hoping
that image may be wiped
clear, that stone
be rolled away,

Our glass shards
blue and yellow, green,
once scattered sill to floor
might up and lift our
cushioned seats -
perhaps we'll climb out windows,,

we ought to go outside,
let's off and find the sun!
There's a world within
and a world without and
here inside there's nothing.
There is nothing inside.
Come in.

we are all still learning how to love, after all these years of being alive

True Story

There's something about war that keeps a soldier's hands unclean.
No matter how many times he scrubbed them,
however many hours he scoured, his hands had still held death.
There's something else about hands that carry guilt;
sometimes they reach for a bottle.

It went like this:
there were four of them to start, until one of them wasn't.
Thus, they were three rambunctious boys
making mud pies in the New York summer sun,
riding bikes and shooting hoops until two of them took up arms.
One of them left for Vietnam, and a part of him didn't come back.

When his body returned, his body turned toward the bottle.
It didn't take long before he struck out and left.
With an Alice pack strapped on his back and blurred vision,
he took to his drink and got gone.
He called a few times, but every call was worse.
He eventually just stopped calling.

He was seeking summer sun, a cheap buck and a pretty girl.
He settled in a couple of times, but his palms were still tack to the touch.
It was like the wrong wrist mixed it's fingers in,
or the right hand cared too much.
It was wise that Pilate washed his clean before the execution.

Now the streets are bursting brilliant,
and the light pours in through windows.
In the stillness of a ticking clock, particles of dust
float onward to settle into corners.
This is not the way things were,
now lift yourself to meet with me,
reverse the flow to feel this out,
and bring it back to center.

Fast forward, the streets are wet.
. or the shadow is split by dim-lit streetlights as you stumble your way from the bar.
.. or the wind is whipping your hair about, and you snuggle more deeply into a scarf.
... or the songbirds sing in lilting uplift and you lean back bright to take it in.
With your fingers twisted about a lover's palm, he asks you for some change.

This time, you were right. He was gonna spend it on booze anyway.
You still sound like an asshole when you say it, but, you were right.
Tonight he will tuck in, laid up on cardboard and wrapped in a sleeping bag,
he will kick the ground clean of syringes and gravel,
sip from a flask and try to remember how to forget.

quit being shitty to homeless folks

Building A Home

Whatever fine fate ought that
I'd love this bunch here,
let ever it be.
I'd have all this the same.
I'd been never enamored as
how soars the skyline,
not streetlights or buildings,
not fortune and fame,
but one day perchance here
and tread on this doorstep -

now everything's different
now nothing's the same

In my stomach which quivers
by my hand's steady shake,
in my heart which spills contents
to bedside and sheets

I am potent and lovely.
I am building a home.

met with mixed results, as is tradition

So Lazy Toward God

It is here in the silence when I see you best -

(funny how one dulled perception
perpetuates the gathering of
others)

though the rain falls to gravel
to filter to ground, drizzling
gutters drop buckets by
street sides,
and in all of this
all I see is you.

You are holding your hand up
to show me your palm, your
fingers stretched upward, so
lazy toward God.

Your eyes are still pleading
and I'm sure,
I'm sure that mine are. I would

reach my hand before me, for
that's the place where you are,
and touch my lines to
wrinkled hand, go
swimming in the sea.

In this rain, I hear you calling:
be love;
I'd be that.
I believe that you'd let me, I do.

Those eyes burn wholes where liars stand
straight through to truth

,, so
see me.

Come looking.

What one's got
the other needs - what one needs
they've got
as much.

why did I write this ass hat so many poems?

Of All Of These

I am no beast, nor
a caster of shadows
lest light fall before &
I stand in the way

(*in which case,*
 blame my body)

Are we birds of a
feather or lightning
rods reaming some
potent affective, some
hole in the ground?

Was i
t all
then
 for no
thing?

I wear this once-human
now found-it-alone,
it was set by the
bedside as if
some unworthy

forgive &
forget me

but I'll not forget you.
I could not forget.

starting to come to grips with heart ache

Home, Child

Your kiss was like blood in shark infested waters,
and my god, they were begging to taste.
I was wrapped in old gauze,
shivering as the waves tore holes
and soaked the tape
that held my coverings.
We were copper seas and the
tide, it taste of pennies.
All our nostrils flared open
in indignant display.
No darkness dare touch
upon our sunken temple,
rations spilled in piles
before our feet,
missing fingers choked on
golden bands, this--
this was our own holy brokenness.
No dreams or terror could tear it apart.
I built these walls, this wall, this pile,
with my own flesh as paper and my own blood as ink.
This soaking mess is the child we bore.
Whether by canal or comforts, tears or torn-up pictures
lit to blazing for moments that fleck and float away,
this is our progeny. You can't take that with you.
We are now bound to leave up out this place
with nothing between us.
I can no more bleed for you
than hasten the sun's up and over.
I can no more go back to
rewrite all the wrongs
than to rethink that evening
when our fingers first touched.
I can no more breathe
when I have offered you my hand
while your fingers fill my rib cage
than I can keep up with
the dreams that you're pursuing.
I can not return
and neither can you.
This is home now, child.
Be here.

dating her sucked so hard, oh my god

Thoughts From The Washtub

She was a warm, smoking gun.

Her hips held swagger that
swayed as they'd rock,
rolling in languish over so
many drawn eyes and raised lashes.

She was a warm apple pie,
and I was aching to try.

In the woods by the path,
the words rolled off easily,
and she lapped them up as had
one or two before her.
High cheeks and whatnot,
true as was told,
but I've grown at least a little
since then.

I've said before that which was told truly,
but I can smell in the air
something humid approaching.
When it comes,
where can I rest my bones
to hide from the storm?
To break from the form
of the mold I was placed in?

pro-tip: don't date people who are naive enough to trust me

These Rainstorms, These

I've been thinking today
about all of this nonsense
pertaining to clouds
and to silver and grey
, all these linings beleaguered
by bouts of depression
, the problems persistent
, the problems that stay.

I think I know what I think now.

I've been watching these
rainstorms, these passers-by
and the sun that was there before them
and the sun that remained thereafter

: there is no more truth
in what is apparent than
what is beside or what
shines behind

: there is no silver lining
: there is no touch of grey

the Sun shines far off before them -
beyond, life pants and makes sweat;

the Sun does not need

mediocre advice: fifty cents

May 6, 2011

I got this itch in my get-up and here I am,
this tiny, frightened monster.
My shoes are worn,
my toes poke through.
I'm not sure where I've been.
It's hard to say.

The whole thing seems brilliantly colored
but absent of dimension.
The whole thing seems brilliant
but the words are all hollow
and I don't know where I'm going.

It seems anymore like my days are made up of footsteps
and movements, patterns and routines
but it was only as long ago as a few layers of skin
when I was a wild and feral creature:
man, and not machine,

and I don't know where I'm going with this.
I ripped up all my clothes off,
ran naked into the storm
but the storm, it stood me out.
The affair just left me muddled,
bloodied, messed up.
but I'm no longer angry and that's something to celebrate.

I don't mind all the manners and the matters at hand
and I don't know where I'm going
but we'll see where I end up.
I have yet to be decided and I've got little but time
, time and energy,
a little bit of space and nothing to prove,
nothing to fear. A few regrets.
I've got patience.
I can do this.
We'll see where this all ends up.

spoken into a voice recorder, date unknown

She Knows Her Name

There are two good things about me
and one of them is you.
The rest is bound to fairy tales
and yesterday, which is no more,
but today
there are two things:

you &
what I do

See,
all those things
you'd see as special
are little more than dimes per dozen,
and talent is not hard to come by.

The difference between
potential and kinetic is
the difference between
broke and the bank,
no more and today,
but

you, my dear,
are motive in succession,
whether real or contemplation
still you offer inspiration.

I don't want to be confusing
so let me spell it out too clear:
there are two good things about me,

when I'm real &
when you're near

spread it on a little thick there, friendo

Kind News, Good Soldier

What if that sea were you? Or me?
Could you just let it be?
or would you wear a cool and calming smile,
bleary-eyed and starving, scared?
What if your true intentions were bared?

To which you respond,
"I walk in the sea, it wants to overtake me."

It's purging maw and gaping jaw
break free from tyrannical diet or form,
bursting, flavors mingling with spit and kisses.
Your lips were quivering with anticipation,
and the soft tread of footfall brought to mind
all the memories of hardwood creaking hallways.

Do you remember when you laid your burden down,
down in the sand or a shifting soil?
Your mouth curled in corners, twisting at
awkward angles, bent and lent to bending
and your lips were quaking, shivering.

Yours was a basin boat floating,
bobbing gently to the rhythm of a heartbeat,
the rocking of the sea.
Your hands balled up in palms -
but before you could squint, the pain, it had vanished!

Lower your guard, good General, sir.
Lower your walls, for I've some kind news!
Raise the standard high, good Brigadier General!
Bear with it favors! and fruits! and good fortune!
Lower your guard, sir, for I've some kind news:

The war is over, good soldier. Come home.

turned out that I butchered military terminology. Fwoops.

The Shelves Of Our Thrifty

The shelves of our thrifty
store second-hand treasures
that dirty-nail vagrants
and blind kids may buff
and make new again.
Make it their own.

Their stained smooth silk
and chipped glass bring a smile
to the bodies suffering &
spirits alight. A light burning
quickly and furious, indignant,
pushes against the night.

Let their temperatures drop
in the cold of the climate!
Let their cool develop to cold,
cold to still cooler,
and settle on blue.

We've a bright light, and it's never stopped burning.

solidarity, not charity

Youth And Beauty

These bricks lay angled as ever they used to,
these chairs just as stiff as before.
Over the course of a time or two healing,
my legs grew to stretch and to bend around corners;
I no longer leap for the sight of a Greyhound.

No brittle dry leaves or crumbling footpath
can call to halt any two fat feet
that are running to safety,
running away.

If the silt was to settle by the break of the morning,
then who could uphold said settling sand?

Two hands and twenty fingers pulled away from the flow,
leaving behind to fall down all that ought to.
Ten toes and the lightning
were the crest
of the peak of a wave
of a moving to somewhere but home,
to anywhere but here.

These leaves and jagged edges,
they yell to me.
Break!

Oh, tidal wave of youth and beauty!
Break and be free of it, free from the stuff!

Youth and beauty,
for your own sake,
be free.

please stop dying so often

The Morning You Got Married

our hearts and sleeves were sleeping thieves
'til morning broke the spell:

sunlight peak through bedroom windows,
rays of shining, bright and colors
peel apart our waking eyes;
fingers clear the crust remains of another night of dreaming.

coffee brewed by blessed timer,
juice is poured &
pants are filled
left to right,
toe to ankle,
knee to thigh,
repeat and buckle,
button up through stumbling doors,
down the stairs to meet the day.

I moan and groan and whisper soft
'til breathing smoke and steaming mug
clear aching lungs by wrenching cough -

"Good morning, love."

Your eyes gaze thick through early fog
and clear your throat to sing response,
as if by angels' sweet repose
your voice compose,

"Good morning, love."

a truck stop waitress kicked me down food and smokes, I wrote this for her

Dishes To Do

Steam and tiny droplets fell hard on her shoulders
and I hoped it would ease all her tension.
She said they were great with the best of intentions,
but so far the most wasn't worthy of mention,
much less than deserving of all that she gave them.
She bathed them, forgave them and kissed all their faces,
erases the crayon and greases the hinges to keep the door swinging,
but again, there were dishes to do.

Her voice, it grew sweeter each time they would meet her,
and theirs were as stale as communion.
I wanted to plead it, my god! You don't need it!
But still, more profound than to witness the sound
of the bending of knees for to help to pay fees
or for alms or alma maters, whichever said souls were more lent to,
or as ever by means of their roots eroding soil
she stiffened her lip and resumed to rolling sleeves,
all aside, there were dishes to do.

Ours was a promise to steer clear the river
or maybe to aim for the bridges.
No trouble can shake me or fat fellow take me,
nor rattle my cage for my cage is no prison
– the padlock is missing –
it's a body sky bound for a greater yet glory
or at least for an end that would make a good story.
I'd travel on outward but inwardly seeking, fast forward or slowly,
either way, there are dishes to do.

her roommates sucked, then she dumped me for my friend

Seated Sores Of Bed Rest

I was smoking then,
thus bent the mile forward
over park bench, pavilion,
a couple of chairs.

There were days left to fashion more
the seated sores
of bed rest and comfort.
Stagnant was a friend to lazy water,
and this here pool is a blight of boot rot.

I'll not be callous to a pruney young plaything,
wrinkle toed and pleasure pressed,
nor beast by measure as held
by like mind.

I've yet to slip to
tighter shackles
than pressing fingers could push
aside.

No cell can hold a soul that can't stop flying.

update: I was wrong, jail cells can definitely stop souls from flying

Train Kids Gone Blooze

short and tall glasses of beer and a bottle
being passed between fingers;
it's almost as though they still had a good time.
laced to his mid-calf and stinking of urine
the bottle be fingers to smooth out some wrinkles.

I've still not forgotten that love were a turnpike,
sharpened and stinging
like eyes in a rainstorm,
puffed up and gleaming
tired of crying, or
tired.

Love's not a plaything
but the trainkids cry loudly
Go-Go Gadget spare change!
A dollar off on donations!

Are you a communist? Because you stallin'…
Don't you believe in change?
Obama does.

got a dollar?

One Fine Day

Sleeping on borrowed bed sheets
by light of love and trepidation,
I was no longer bound by mere immortality.

It was another day of restless lover
followed by a night of flirting,
playful tease and flitting lashes,
whistle sound and speaking rhythm
to the undertow of all we touch and all I'm seeing.

I'm safe for now, but all I know
is called upon in timely manner
once the moment's come and gone.

Now and then I catch a glimpse with squinting eye
but one fine day I'll wrap my arms about her
chest and round to back,
all light and airy fluid motion -
time then slow and calm its clutching.

One fine day I'll find and love her,
she to me and lay me down.

written using a cheap flip-phone in 160 character bursts

The Difference Between

The water is coming,
quick, take your clothes off!
Rain is falling, dance it in with me!
Lift your voice and swing higher,
higher!

Storm cloud!
Rain, come!
Come down!
Down here!

Kick those silly shoes off,
come on and let your hair down!
Storm cloud!
Rain down, the sound, the head pound!
Rain down, rain down!

we saw a storm cloud at the end of a drought, laughter ensued

She Is Not Mine

Oh, but here I sit again!
Again, within these rum soaked walls
and leaking windows,
turning wheels and flicking wrists,
burning alive to bear a way.

And you! You were the most of it!
The bulk of all that I'd deemed worthy!
You! As a golden, secret stair you did lift your legs
and move to him, that cyclic crow!
Him! the caustic catalyst that burned and bore a hole
that rends a whole to many bits.

Ah, but here I sit again,
and nothing but a key or switch might find me
breathing, dreaming, moving forward -
I was a child, and she was a child,
but I am a woman, and she is not mine,
nor mine to judge as my soul might wish to.

self-note: check your sexist clinginess circa 24, kiddo

Will Is Iron, Bed Is Dust

I woke up this morning to dog tongue
informing me a shit is quickly needed.
I shrugged boy awake
and he cleared dreams from eyelids.

Last night I cleared the ground of gravel
and slept naked in my covers.
We snoozed to the smell of woodsmoke, licked nostrils,
and a home bum rewarmed canned goods and white box.
On a town run yesterday we missed a good fella -
NS runner with boxcars open.
Food is probably better though, this water too,
and napkins etcetera so worry be gone.

Boy gets water while I watch our packs in waiting,
writing then to marking records,
calling in to lay the tracks out.
Drizzle drops are soaking through
but camp is high and dry.

Whiskey's strong,
a flask here stronger,
will is iron, bed is dust.

DIIGS: Damn, I'm In Georgia Still

The Wrongs I've Done

I know the sound of New York dying,
her dim-lit streets and boulevards dance
to the whisper of a dusty jazz record.
Her lips sing songs in a step behind rhythm,
words landing angular in pools of squared reflection -
        money, meanwhile, simply takes a taxi.

I'd throw my jacket in the mud for you,
but I trust I'd never see it back... besides,
why bother plugging leaks in cold water flats?
I'd gladly drop bills to bring out old galoshes!

We've got no need for windows or shelving,
not with so many records I've yet to listen to!

      (
      two turntables spin turnstiles glowing
pink and stinking light pollution that roars above the city.
)

Now Pack Rat and Free turn to sleep inside garage doors,
and tomorrow we'll go search for a fix or a solution.

I've lit another cigarette - I'll let this one burn,
and I've got no apologies for the wrongs I've done
that never hurt you.

You may sleep in as you wish to,
for tomorrow I'll find my way.
You may go as ought the wind blows,
or burn through fields
to prove your point.
I pray for you a useful measure,
one day you build a better home.

I've got no time for silly games
nor calls for whose cock's bigger, nor time at all,
see I left my alarm by the railroad in Richmond.

Now the dawn is broke
and my feet have wandered.
I'll soon see to Altman,
and we'll drink whiskey and beer,
singing songs like old New York,
and I'll never apologize for the wrongs I've done
that never hurt you.

sometimes going to Roanoke is a good idea, I assume

Pawn, Be Moved

Let it blow and ring aloud
a loud and billowing stiff breeze
which bends the bone toward arthritic ends,
some sort of unkempt middle ground
surrounded by lush greenery that adds to grey scenery,
dull in its touch.

May was her birthright, April her burden.

You understand, I know you do.
Your skin and sagging flesh pursue the same as mine,
but now -

what for the boredom?
What to do with the freedom paid for by blood and loss?

Once the fingers pinch the pawn,
the pawn be moved by unseen fingers,
holy fingers, sacred tendons,
ten thousand tendrils flooded by selfish motives,
ugly brains with pretty hair,
flowing locks and
higher cheekbones.

Peel the skin from sky-clad bodies,
torn bikinis from two-piece girls,
bear away the ensuing layers, the teenage glory.
Rend no more the powders, creams and lotions
into false visage, mirror-type fallacies
of make-up and hair,
the truth behind the masks we wear

translation: I would like to come out as trans now but, actually, gimme six more years

Yarn And Glue

there's a bridge between two lying eyes
of which each holds
a secret -
one is a tale I may never tell,
the other's made of yarn and glue:

it came swelling from the ground up,
my hands too
          slow to
stop the flow,
now rising tide and
bits of sand surround my knees.

It's getting deeper.

firstly I was singing songs,
some were true and
others gaining.
once I saw the water coming
my shoes got kicked and
tossed aside,
socks peeled down past
arch and toe.

I dipped my feet in,
calves came nextly,
then to naked,
on to under.

I was swept up in the moment
but like a breeze that's
bent to billowing,
I found myself beside the shore
choked with dreams
and begging for more.

being a responsible capitalist makes me want to die

Each One Still

My book was written in dusty roads
by stick as pen, as inkless pen, which
worked for then but was soon
forgotten. I was lead and day
was paper - life was love but now,
years later, hair and beard
but bard is growing into woman
to be a lover. At once, I loved her!

Lend an ear to rose that's
falling, drooping as the summer wilts.
As you will or as you were,
either way, the earth's still
spinning, grinning like from
ear to ear, and god is empty,
hollow space.

Kiss my face and hold me
tender, better now than
then or never. Lap the
licks up, then remember:

Children speaking
Spanish are speaking
Korean too, or English,
Finnish, Russian, other...

Each one still, they need their mother.

for my mother, Theresa

Patience, Love

patience love,
patience,
these things can
only stay broken
so long -

there comes yet
a time, a daybreak
when a healing
smooths over the broken,
the chapped and
worn out,
the spots where
love
took a slap and
a beating.

there comes yet a
time, only
you'll never see it.
you'll only know once
it has come

update: things are still fucky, more to come

Paper Burning Yellow

It was the sound of mothers laughing,
breathing deep as small ones splashed
naked in a pool of lapping bathtub,
their hair be subtle striping held up limp
by shampoo and dreaming.

Soap in eyes and tearful start ups,
bikes that fell and scratching knees. A kiss
and blow could soothe their aching, burning fever
or any else.

We'd had a time to contemplate,
let clouds pass by as rabbits, faces, ghosts -
it all made sense when the world was shown us,
we the world and bow or curtsy.
Fix your hair and clean your ears but be yourself,
what that may be.
Whatever thing or life that be,
by standard high or niche you fall to, cling it close and
don't let go!
No matter what, no, don't let go!

Soapy bodies singing stars that twinkle bright like fireflies,
bits of paper burning yellow, ash to dust and dust to dust.
Soon then came the pretty girls
(I'd pushed her down a year ago!)

We'd grown a hair,
first here then there,
then all the glowing summer days
and school days off to sled outside turned to Nintendo
then to cell phone.

Oh, but what of what we're taught
between the snacks and naps and stories?
Has it all gone wrong,
Or have we only forgotten?

being a grown up is a terrible idea

Took To The Streets

I want for our children to
grow in a world
that is better by far
than the one you were
born to,
the same one as me.
I'm in love with you,
because I am in love with myself

Your gun may be shining,
glinting as steel &
ready to kill
but my heart is the stronger
and I still believe
that the pen stroke
might blow your
cannons to
peaces.

He tilted his head left,
listened,
replied, and the
tear gas was
fired.

We took to the streets.

good ol' fashioned class warfare

For Water And Thinking

I do not fear death but
welcome her,
held at arm's length
or at least just a
pen hand away.

I spent too much time
with a gun in my mouth
and a noose
'round my neck
to now fear
what I begged for
before.

I've pictured death as a lover in waiting,
or a squatter who won't pay my bills.

I've painted as death on the walls of my room
in the dark 'til the sun came
and called me.

I drew death as a breath that was
musty and stale
as if some saltines
sat too long in a pantry -
now I'm dying for water
and thinking:

I've pictured death only as still life.

I stared into the void, the void stared back, the void blinked so I got to punch the void in the arm.

A Borrowed Lighter

Now love, I've got no more than you,
nor nerve to stare at the sun.
My fingers too tremble at the touch of skin
to tender, blessed, righting hands.

My stomach leaps to hear your voice
and a calm settles into my soul.
As if only to know that you're real
and you're here, whether
whatever to lengths and proximity,
I breathe and
I read and
it passes the time.

You were dancing then too,
and your hips,
they swayed singing
and your voice matches mine.

Were your body subtle arches,
I might rest and let my feet up.
Lest I be counted a fool,
ought not I drink up what you'd pour me?
I've thought before and spoken aloud
that all I'd found was null and void,
then comes a booming thunderclap
by means of a
borrowed lighter.

You said your name,
our fingers touched.
Our blessed, righting hands to clasping,
out my number,
out my name.

My fingers tremble to point pressed forward.
Worth the while. Worth the wait.

it's easy to idealize someone with whom you have spent minimal time

At The Mission On 9th Street

I slept all night on
my back to visions of
sugared plums and his
quilt
was a
flag, red-white-and
        blue.
Some woman, she
        left, so
he left as
she'd left him,
        leaving only:

one pair of pants
one sweatshirt
        navy blue
a grey glove and
rolling papers.

He woke up or
never slept – I turned
to him sitting there,
arms around his knees
staring at the wall.
        I wanted to ask,
Are you feeling okay?
Are you needing to talk?
        Instead, it was
'hey buddy' --
that's it.

He was gone when I woke,
they made us
get up quickly to
count all our heads -
he was gone,
got up in the night
and left like
she left him, and
now he can never come back.

He's here to get his clothes.

winterin a homeless shelter in Joplin Missouri, a few months before the big tornado hit

Sidewalk By A Greyhound

the sidewalk by a greyhound
a man greets another
says his car won't start.
　　　　what year's it?
oh-seven
　　　　she's a beaut-
thanks, just got 'er

　　　　gotcher keys?

　　　　　　　- sip of tea
　　　　　　　two men walk by
　　　　　　　conversing Italian;;

thanks a lot, pal
　　　　not a problem,
　　　　sign right here.

a girl with blond
hair pops her head out a
window, watches
like we do.
a pigeon struts toward me,
darts to the
left, weaving through
feet and unoccupied
pavement
she
　　　　tsktsk
her
tongue to
the roof of her
mouth
calling her
pigeon

come here.

imagine 'tsktsk' sounding like how you would call a cat, tongue to teeth – yes, like that

Once Our Shoes Are Off

I guess I want to be your ride home.
Not because you owe it to me,
or I want to be above you,
but because that's where you're going.
I'd like to be there too.

I'd like to wrap my arms about you,
yours as much 'round me,
to kiss you once our shoes are off,
to place them by the door.

I know that you've got things to do
and tomorrow's just as busy,
but for just tonight could we brush our teeth,
could we stay up late to talk?

I'd like to see the ceiling move,
to rumble toward the stairs.
That's us, you know:
bright lights burning up.
I'd like to spend some time with you.

It's all I've got, time and patience;
I'll give you that
and the other I'd share with you freely.

she actually turned out to be kind of a jerk

Soothe My Soul

thank you lord
for tea leaves,
how they warm and
soothe my soul
on this long and boring evening
bent to small, the
morning
hours
take their toll, now
I've got something
to keep me up, alert
or somewhat conscious
      even as the seconds pass
      to a third and into
      minutes:
these leaves inside
silk satchels
how they warm and
soothe my
soul

riding Greyhound sucks, but rooibos tastes like creamsicles

Simple, Glowing Truth

Once I'd bit to morsel, I
licked my lips to savor flavor
        passed to tongue by honeyed finger
                only to suckle dry days later

        but those were days my blood was racing!
        eyes were cast to trodden sandals,
                rainbow shoes that danced a jig --

the resulted stumbling footsteps
then confessed to flattened arches

Now I see the sun a'rising,
        clouds that sully bright horizon
        burst with silver jewelry lining!

As was once and henceforth always
birds were chirping sing-song sages
        prone to preening -

        I, by gleaning,
        learned a simple, glowing truth:

        if you're not in control of your life,
        then your life is out of control.

for a low, low monthly fee, I will tell you how to live your life

That Scarf You Wore

Slurping sweet kisses from a syrupy well
was a day well spent by the standard of my mind's eye -
      many days could pass by
      by the time I'd retire to a swelling
            swollen lip throbbing love
            and compassion
      to the thrashing of my chest inside my sweater,
      your mouth against mine.

      Ours were pink and pale
            while others smiled darker hues -

      long and thin or pursed and puckered,
      lips were want to beg to taste
      to touch the corners of your chin bordered smile.

You were beautiful under covers,
      but that scarf you wore did something to me,
      something else entirely

she was a cutie who eventually liked hippies more than punks

A Pit Or Shell

don't touch me
with your
fingertips, I
want the whole damn things in,
all of 'em ripping
pulling apart these lungs
and vein 'til
all that's left is a pit or shell
        the little bit where
        the words all pass off
&   the breathing slows 'til
        all I've got is this,
        is nothing

there's no sugar coathing it, this is about getting my asshole finger-blasted

Spilled By Bedsides

This, my crutch -
my fist, my crutch;
this tobacco and fruit,
this pipe,
this crutch;
my legs were both loathsome
my brow dripping sweat
        so my toes took to pedals
bicycle! my crutch

o this brimming of issue, the cough in my lungs
o that scurrying car park, that house on the hill
o that narrowing sound as it blast through my ears
o this harrowing morning that burst into tears

        o joyous!
        o laughter!
for rage spilled by bedsides,
you lifted my insides!

        now I'm wrapped up
        in gauze tape, my
        bones showing thru
        and the end is beside me:

I limped for my crutch.

losing the ability to walk is a weird experience

Eyes Closed And Wanting

Goose pimpled skin led to shivering flesh
   as degrees gave way to grey skies
         & falling eyes.
      a tumultuous tide could roll across
      then recede from whence it came
   for where springs tide but from time?

      It has no home.

hers were digits that counted the seconds
that passed between the fingers between us

tiny, forceful stems burrowing.
greying and gone, the moment gave to seconds,
    measurable units fading fast and faster,
      waiting for the sun to sigh
      or to sell the farm,
      the family home.

by way of hear and tell,
    the moment was finite
    but it may have never ended
if only I'd kept my eyes closed and wanting

divorce is really, really hard

So Death Will See

look at this
this mess of homes
and all her thousand aching arms
are reaching round
a rotting stump
these insects are angry to see me
there is a hollow calm
not of peace
but of void
and her upset arms
still they aim toward me
how they hide beneath a
blanket of broken limbs
of crying trees
they border this meadow
and weep of their saplings
they run as if tear drops
they form on this road
she was once something beautiful

but like unto
life that will
make itself happen
so death too
will see things
through

a beautiful forest hike opened to a clear cut; hillside we cried in silence and wrote poems

Drunk With Laughter

I spent two long months there -
it now seems so trivial.

The day in, day out as the sun's up and down
             was time to smooth the fading scars.
             It's not as though two puffy eyes
                    were red or gleaming
                    with demons of former relations

Now ever as yesterday, today is tomorrow,
the day we've been crying about since the sun rose

The beaten path was gravel road
             and we pissed beside it
             drunk with laughter, drinking beer.
       Hands were holding golden rod,
             heads all laurel, leafy crowns

       Hers were pointed, cresting toes
       Hers were songs sung catlike, dreamy

We were little more than nothing:
puffs of smoking cigarettes

some things seem less special before you eventually begin to miss them

Buffalo By Train Tracks

I spent a few years
dying of hunger, though
      my belly was fat,
      my gullet was full
and I spent those days
crying
my ears wet with dew
- they were pressed to the ground
and listening for daybreak

My eyes were both red
with the flame of a hell
I no longer believed in,
bursting with demons
that long to break free

I hoped that the nightfall would
let loose her locust
to fly in my window,
to take me away.
That night never came.

luckily for this book, the trigger doesn't pull itself

No One Has Mentioned Him

It was 20 to nine, I had five minutes left,
tossed on my boots, smoked my last cigarette.

There's a man at the mission,
he smells something awful, a
mixture of piss and fear.

He's sat on that bench all day every day
since I've been here.
He hasn't come to meals
or chapel, has no bed.

No one has mentioned him.

I've thought to ask a dozen times, does he eat?
He just sits there, stinking like piss.

I said it tonight, 'sleep well, brother,'
the first words I've said to him.
Five days at the mission,
the first words I've said to him.

He didn't respond.

No one has mentioned him.
No one's said a word.
It's all our own problems,
I'm disabled, I can't work,
that woman's a bitch,
no one likes her, she works here.

He just sits there.
The left sleeve of his
coat, the top, it falls down.
He lifts it back up,
he just sits there
in his sandals,

in the snow, in the cold,
he just sits there and stares.

I've thought a dozen times to ask, does he eat?
No one has mentioned him.

humans are terrifying animals

Light On Two Coffee'd Bodies

I'm wrapped in something new
It's the thing which I've been looking for for
so much of my life, and now that it's here
I run free into cities and play with a dog,
drink kombucha and wine to incense and falafel.
There are birds in the trees and the rain's
not yet pouring.

The sun is out and I'm smiling.
The sun is out and I can hardly believe it.

There was night for so long,
was no sun to be seen. I was
hurting, and I couldn't see where I should run to.

Like the point just before the sunrise
where the outlines are forming, light
where was darkness and ghosts gaining faces- well,
that was New York.

As I say, the sun is out now.

The moon is at 3:30 and the first ribbon dances,
it's haze in a fog but it's brilliant diminish.
You hold your hands out in front of you to
see your fingernails
and it may not be true,
but you swear that you see them.
The sun is coming.

Turn your head-
there are mountains and valleys but
sunlight is peaking as a most sincere voyeur
to fill up our trousers (the outsides)
        and gleaming.
The sun's hanging high in blue up and out,
it sheds light on two coffee'd bodies who are
waiting for the night to come.

It all builds up the way that it ought to,
I have no doubt in that.
I do wonder though where it will end.

just moved to Portland… maybe, 25?

Turned To Gold

So what do I
do when I've
swallowed the
sun?
I am
bursting and
gorgeous but
don't wanna burn
up.
When my body's a
star, my god,
what do stars eat?
Now all of
my tendons
glow brilliant and
hostile.
Now all of my
veins turned
to gold.
I've got
no defined
contours,
a puddle of sun.

Am I
still yet a
woman when I've
floated

away.

The One And Two

What, apart from death and dying,
wraps about a twisted finger
like at least
just once a day,
right before the sun starts setting?

Mine were gnarled, mangle digits
counting out the one and two,
the moment there
where blue goes grey,
then fades to black.

Press the tip back, count it loudly -
now to do the dishes piled.

writing silly shit after dinner but I was also on dish duty soon

Rock Hill Morning Growing

My knobby knees were shaking
by the dawn of the daybreak
on the floor inside a semi
by the two foot, ten gear shifter.
I'd been sending a signal and it was carried by a tower,

Light was peering through windows,
sneaking glances, bright and blue.
Just yesterday a woman called to mention her contractions,
and this Rock Hill morning growing?
Let's just say it never happened.

hitch hiking is okay sometimes, but South Carolina sucks at all times

Skin From Tender Fingers

So, I'm singing in the streets again and
dancing 'tween my fingers. A cigarette is
lit and burning, but no remorse
or coursing,
bleeding, punching,
pulling, peeling skin from tender fingers,
live and loaded
like you mean it, lovely.

What are you calling love or burning?
It was nothing but domestication,
cats that sing and kiss in rhythm
to the tune of washing dishes
or pillow talk and dreamy kisses

beats the shit out of me, I was pretty drunk when I wrote this

Next To Next

There it goes, and
then it's gone
and on and on
through next to next
and it's turtles all the way down -
goodness too,
'cause I don't know
when I'll grow to grieve it.

Railcar passings,
road dogs come and road dogs go -
you never know
but today
I can be pretty sure.

Tigger too (Stormy three)

I'll Breathe Smoke

Goodness, but a train is a saintly, drunken sport!
Dark and dreamy, and a butt-flap kept my
pants from tearing. Solitude is hard to find, a
moment clean to clear the clutter forming. I'm glad
for it - he's a good kid and his chest is lovely.
Hairy though and peeping through.
Kiss me twice through telephone, and
I'll breathe smoke and wait some more.
Patience is easy, it's the waiting that's hard.

waiting for rideable trains going the right way takes so fucking long

Never Go Hungry

The silence was louder than some other more audible.
Your words could not have made me listen
and your hands would be fallen on deafer ears.
I can hear you.
I hear you.

I am grateful to hear you and look forward to
meeting you,
seeing you,
being you.
Welcome home dear friend,
we've waited so long.

These are the markings we allow to push ahead.
We turn down the noise and spill our spirits across a bedside table.
Kiss them goodbye every time that you see it
and you'll never go hungry again.

I talk a lot, but some folks talk a lot a lot

Sleep Removed

Today is but a sleep removed
from yesterday or tomorrow.
The day's the same and sun is shining,
a little brighter and glowing by increasing measures.

I kissed a girl who'd love to meet me
and another who thinks she might know.
I'd twist her hair in tight little curlings,
her body as shorn or as sweaty as mine,
and we wriggle in bedsheets while a pup hogs the blankets.

The movie was nice but the company better,
and dinner was somewhere in between.

I mean really, everyone loves curry.

for Percy & Pan, who opened me to new kinds of magick

Thin Fingers

remember thin sleeves passed between thin fingers,
woven by fingers of Chinese wages?
pull as you ought to,
pull as you might
thin sleeves would become
the more tight
as you pull, and
your fingers might
swell up and bruise.

Remember the moment we loosened our grip?
the sleeve fell limp and
thin fingers were freed.

(toy finger traps)

Seine, Where We Fell

Here was where she fell inside
her bodice dripping, soaked and clinging -
here was where it came together
an afternoon so drenched by hues of
golden, gilded sun-lit droplets
rays of streaming glory! glory!
held her hand for mine to hold,
I swallowed hard to take the lump
should Lord herself, by sweet repose
or tender prose give grant to marry!

Here was where she fell inside,
and I there too did follow suit -
her cherry lips and hazel eyes,
they bore and bear a beaming tarry,
hand in hand and eye to eye.
Should ever lovely come to bury
each day was worth the lonely while!

Ring to fingers, eyes were tearing,
crying Yes! My love, I'm falling!
Catch me soft and hold me tender,
thus each day I'd loving tend her,
her to me and soul to soul
and this is where we fell inside
by the bank of the blue of the Seine.

regarding a character in 'A Sunday on La Grande Jatte' by Georges Seurat

Young Girl's Gullet

The thirst was something different though, and
hardly more than empty pages.
Words and scrawling epitaph
could coat the walls with glory story -
This one's bound for old New Yorker!

A song to lift a lilting spirit,
A tune to tone a creaking hinge,
a door knob open gently, gently

Even as the sun was setting,
songs were sung to passers by,
change or no, a nod or greeting.
Please to put a penny in the young girl's gullet.

A beer would do me sweetly now, but food?
That's easy.

dumpsters are often full of food, but rarely full of booze

Keep To The Way Home

Here and now, about this time,
but never any later than would be less than appropriate -

here about the center now,
the wheels may cough and spin around,
breaking time and bounding forward
into space and out of mind.

still and silent, your
quiet, guarded fences
call for Braille-studded armor troops
but know best to not expect too much, save for
shuffled feet and calm diversion.

smile a breath and breathe it a while,
let out the better
but keep to the way home.

also, cough syrups should not be used recreationally

Eulogy For Grandma Bills

Your rosy hue, now deathly blue,
sings symphonies to me.
Your aura, now engulfed somehow
by dreams of tide and sea,
can rest in peace as time will cease
its morbid fascination,
and may your end now bring a bend
in city, state and nation

for my great grandmother, Norma Bills, at her funeral when I was 12

Raise A Toast

Amidst the trees and bending knees,
I see myself bereft
of any strength and crying hard;
I'm all that I've got left.
Here I lay upon the ground
and needing for someone
to kiss me soft, explain it all,
they'd never quite be done.

burn the trees and bend the knees
live and die the way you please

Amongst the pleas and pending fees.
I've seen a better place.
I know some unseen higher hand
may reveal some unseen face,
a bigger man, a better plan,
a reason for the night -
but is the meaning some unfeeling
parting of the light?

plant the trees and mend the knees
it's all the same, it's all the same

So here's to the tears and the times that we both cried!
And here's to the fears and the times that we both lied!
Lift a glass, raise a toast!
Cut a wrist, who bleeds the most?
If we're still in love,
then why the hell does this hurt so bad?

unfinished song about my first girlfriend when we should have broken up

How To Let Go

I came to your window,
but you weren't there.
You came to my mind,
but you're not here.
It's not the face, or the drinks,
or the memory that's killing me.

It's the dreams.
The serpent ridden dreams.
Should I hang the dream catcher up
like the fool I well may be?
and what is killing me?

is it seeing this fools past
in dimensional reality?
is it seeing her face again?
or is it something else?

I'm so nervous, I can't stop shaking my legs

don't text your ex, don't text your ex, don't text your ex, circa 18 years

Abhayagiri Bound

deep within this mind that's turning
is a fire that keeps burning
leaf and twig and tree and life;
ignore it more and pay the price.

,, andso

goodbye! so long! farewell! adieu!
(this sort of thing I say to you
as rocket launch and bullet's crash
bid goodnight from under ash)
A long, eclectic midnight game
plays it's course and feels no shame.
A tear is shed, a bus is gone -
this little girl will be someone.

excited to go to a Buddhist monastery, circa 17 years

Free Until They Return

To a world that's left me nothing -
I know you finally!
You are nothing to fear. It has melted away.

It was wrong of you to try -
not that you would care,
but just the same, I see your flaw,
and in that sighting my perception changes

This life is but a series of daily chances,
(most never seen)
to be taken up or given up,
I've thrown my cares to the wind, and
I'll be free until they return again.

if I don't feel manic currently, I must be all better, circa 14 years

To Give Up Hope

i
I wonder if you see me;
in all of this, we've both gotten uglier,
and blindness seems to be a fashion statement.
Could a claim of sanctuary evolve into romantic entanglement?
Look into these eyes, and for a moment
(but only that moment)
we see

ii
The weight of years spent on fruitless investments -
it's enough to tear the fabric of a life only I can see.
So as for this lie I've been living,
how does one give up on happiness?

iii
To give up on the wind
and all of it's obscurities, but can I?
There are endless, fruitful possibilities
and I've seen them;
for once, something is real and it's mine

iv
So now I'm giving in -
this is too much like yesterday to not do so.
and in all of this I'm fine, as I've rarely seen myself,
and here in this place everything is alright...
(to give up hope is liberation
and to deny you is to accept myself)
but if everything changes
and adaptation is the key
then where is the door?

let's cut the shit, being a teenager was awful

My First Poem

If I were to die tomorrow
would I let you know?
If I were to die tomorrow
would that chariot swing low?
Would you miss me while I'm gone?
Wondering where we went wrong?
If I were to die tomorrow...

written in third grade, I was promptly sent to the guidance office

Storm Is King

...and we all know that the storm is king
as a black sensation, cessation of all feeling.
Sorrowful tunes and tones trimmed in gold
serve as a tome for the hours passing by,
greeting the day with an unsurmountable feat:
the pitter patter of the footfalls of children.

my toddler nieces were going to wake up any minute

Breathing River Flow

My fingers are made of meat and sinew,
grasping concepts and illuminating words.
They reach to yours and weave between them,
fingers locked in breathing river-flow.

Your hands are small, but they fit in mine.
I too am afraid to jump this cliff, but I'll do it -
I've done it, I'm doing it now.
I know better than read to encircling iris,
dilated pupils taking notes in the sand.
It's all over now and we've barely begun.

I see you, I'll know you
but I'll wait for better weather.
Your cheeks will warm and dry,
and the last tear will fall -
it's then I'll be there for you.

a love poem on mushrooms about someone also on mushrooms

Self Unimportant

What but a trial could travel the length
of the distance still needed to give myself strength?

What but the pain of a day worth repeating
could challenge my heart to continue it's beating?

Who in a calm but a questioned intention
brings to the light what's not worthy of mention?

To consider the chances, the stroke of a pen
loses significance when held to magnificence.
Of all of the times and the trials of days
when held to the light of a grander scheme
seem to lose grip; the don't hold such a sway
when my eye catches glimpse at invisible themes

a smashing together of several short poems from high school

Silver Lining

Look to the trimmings
of the Architect's soul -
silver and gold.

They're silver and gold
and the nonchalant efficiency
of their drive-by showering
renders respect in the coldest
of hours, the cool
of their showers.

there I go again, talking about clouds and shit

Thoughts On God Nature

i
can't find it, can't fake it, can't give it, can't take it
can't give up my life to a cause that's unknown
I'll never get in if I don't get the ticket
I never will reap if I never will sow

ii
Taste the heat, and smell the rain
Hear the thoughts and feel the pain
Take revenge and thus play god
Take a bow, it's your applause

iii
Spinning on our axis, revolve around the sun
Now we bow or curtsy, fear before the one
Lacking grace and twist of spine
Show respect for all divine

some of us get caught up in weird shit early

A Couple Of Hours

I dreamed of a day when I let the past die -
come conscious daylight, though, no one can fly.
We breathe and dream but in a couple of hours
we wake up to realize things have gone sour,
and in a couple of hours we're drained of our power,
a couple of hours.

I let loose a flower to fall to the ground,
unshakable, certain that it would be found.
She breathed and dreamed but as she turned her head
she realized that cold dirt would work for a bed,
and for a couple of hours we're drained of our power,
a couple of hours.

I had an encounter reflecting intelligence,
cold calm cried out for relief of my loneliness.
Writing and twisting, I pulled from the ashes
something that sways over most of the masses,
but for a couple of hours they're drained of their power,
a couple of hours.

my first attempt at punk lyrics, circa 23 years

One Way Or Another

How many times, I sought to seek,
have life and love found ground to keep?
How many forlorn dancers strange
have seen a home so out of range?
Who's found a calm and cooling quench
where hardened souls have sensed a stench?

In hearth and home, heart and head -
some aptly soft, though never dead -
so seldom seen has one such soul
professed to have a common goal.

The stakes too high, the price too steep,
to many promises to keep;
an all around surefire plan
can soothe a soul or char the hand

translation: how can I keep being weird and also not be lonely

A Note On My First Kiss

How lovely it was - our shivering flesh,
our hands entwined with steaming breath.
We told the truth of both our lives -
we knew nothing could take that night.
I love you, all that could be spoken
with your head on me and my thoughts unbroken.
Of all that I say, I know just this:
nothing will end that casual kiss.

she kissed me because I admitted to not having kissed yet

Crow On A Power Line

My darling, my beauty,
I miss you already!
It was a nonchalant moment
when you
whisked me away!

(and my darling!
how hard you make this to write!)

You perched upon the wiry,
silhouetted inspiration -
of the crystalline endeavors,
I cannot bear to try!
For you, my black
silk beauty, are a gift, more,
from the Goddess herself!
Yet even as I etch this
inky black epitaph,
I cannot help but to notice, my dear,
that you are no longer here.

she was a shadow on my desk from the electric line outside of math class, circa 13 years

Soliloquy In The Key Of F

Such a silly girl!
Your fears, all unfounded,
will flutter and fall
once your feet are firmly grounded!
To fret over feeling of no consequence -
a fool's sort of freedom
that's lacking at best.
What could result but to conquer or fail?
The latter's the chapter fought off tooth and nail.
In any event, the result matters little
as long as this veering brings me towards the middle.

temporarily renamed to 'Soliloquoy In The K Of Alan' for a kid I met who killed someone

On A Blanket Of Leaves

You!
> in a burning mass of stringy hair
> unshaved pits and
> sweaty scalps
>> in a bantering dialogue
>> more so closed than all the doorstep
>> you sleep beside might-

You!
> and here about this mess of faces
>> all entwined, enraptured faces
>> picketing smiles and
>> lying eyes
> could bear the breeze
> and walk away

there's something about Haight-Ashbury hippies that annoys the shit out of me

Walk Around

Strong black coffee and a cheap cigarette -
a bitter breakfast but I take what I can get.
Turn the spoon and overturn,
turn around and overtake,
      take away , take away & walk around.

Thick black Bible and a way to forget
a bitter memory but I haven't got there yet.
Take the lead and lead us through,
drop the reins and drown a while,
      fake a smile , fake a smile & walk around.

Long black winter and an old karmic debt
a bitter woman is now an angered suffragette.
Seize the day and stay it out,
out of mind and out of town,
      tear it down , tear it down & walk around

Break the mold and bust a jaw,
tell the people what you saw,
      walk around , walk around , walk around

unfinished song that I can sing, but I haven't heard the music yet

Thought On Snow

Snow has always felt
like such a strong-armed
home intruder as it
covers up the
treetops and the
hillsides by the
bucket, but
        watch:

that lowly peasant,
mass of dirt
stands true to space -
        this place is mine -
& highbrow flakes
make weak and dripping
shed from branch
to melt away
or off to stream
to creek and gully,
river, sea,

it was the first time that I had seen Wolf Creek with a blanket of snow

From A Basement In Nebraska

three were snow covered,
glorious keys played softlike and
        plucking strings wore holes in shoe soles,
        laces dangled by the curbside
        toes each tucked near tongue and eyelets,
            dreaming of the further on
                when things will be magical,
                    things will be grand.

        two were singing songs
            off/note and sipping from mason jars
            of lovely, my lover, my -

            two were born elsewhere
            and neither the same
            but neither like these two
        two were some strangers to scenes like these.

one was a lost soul,
the others were ready
        or the rest we all goners,
        but him?

        He'll be fine.

she invited us to stay but didn't mention us to her parents or her parents to us

On Our Trip To Peru

We were a moonstruck duet,
bound to a washtub basin boat
      and bobbing in the water.
      Dangling slivers of tree branch fingers
          swept and scrape the surface,
      wave hello as we pass
      goodbye up ahead

At once and again your afghan slipped
      baring skin to brutal cold,
      and more than once
      our dark friend smiled and sank
      as if to nod in approval

      , as it were with midnight eyes
      bright skies part ways by the path
and our shining was through for a day.

wherein I dreamed that we got along better than we did

All That I Could See

long before the day seemed worthy,
she was all that I could see!

in a manner befitting more the mien
        of bird or birch or
        trembling finger,
she was bigger than her body
but born to it the same.

She pressed the breeze with
 raised fingers
up

blew a kiss and
part the sea

she was sacred to me, and I think that I may always love her

Shush.

the words and dots connect
themselves to silhouette
my shadowed frame, my
darkened figure reaching
                out,
as if
any stroked ego meant more
than ego stroked and
shining:

shush.
the radio's off,
and there are no more distractions
except this glass of wine
                and the mug I poured my chips in
                had coffee left, but just a bit

and these margins are awful,
                        this paper's a mess,
                        and I've finished the wine -

my, but that didn't take long

note to self: being wine drunk is more fun than reading about it later

Good Intentions (The Best)

I guess we're never quite sure of ourselves, are we?

We roam this sphere with the best of intentions,
wary of pitfalls and mudslides,
sinking to the deepest to rid ourselves of this
nagging fear of failure.
Perhaps it has been selfish or foolish this whole time,
but all the while,
but these damn good intentions!

Nestled away in the comforts
a plethora of insecurity and delusion
It's a wondrous invention I'll surely assert -
deftly accurate and
positively daft.

born about a mid-July's splendor,
glorious colors and humid air,
we rested our souls and ate of
a bountiful plenty.

don't speak for fear to ruin,
bursting in all the corners
of all the facets
of all our minds

Be still. There is no God.

this is the first page of the first hardbound journal I purchased

Posthumous Prequel To Day 2

birds and calling them -
bits of chewed bubble gum &
burning, lit cigarettes made of
pre-smoked tobacco.
        I'm writing now by
mental menthol,
minty morning smiling eyes
a sleepy grin between my ears

most of my daily journaling has been this kind of garble

Hair And Flesh Alike

To live is dancing flicker flames
that reach and touch to open wounds,
        burning hair and flesh alike

        firstly I was tearing skin
        flicker flames that made no sense
                then came teasing motion steps
plus mine were feet that added rhythm

        drums played fingers
        that bled a break beat -

snap your fingers,
        snap your neck

translation: shit's confusing

Coming Up Flowers

It's all coming up flowers in this city of roses,
be it nighttime or daylight, pleasure or pain.
There were moments held aching,
coddle clothes curled up snuggling
(no, I'll never away) to
burn cardboard and wood chips.

I'll tell you my story,
I've showed you my soles.
They're grey and greying, and
soon they'll be gone.
Once my shoes fall to pieces,
then you'll find me on the floor.

moving into a house after being homeless for an extended period is weird

Four Months Later

The view from my window is a
bland one, but
precious to me.

It's my portal to the world outside
      after I've locked myself in

      The leaves rustle along the ground,
      tossed here and there
      by a playful breeze -

        squirrels
dance
      through
  ladder
    steps

laughing at the absurdity of it all.

I used to think that
I could be a victim
     as well as a victor

but sometimes
a girl must gather up her strength
     and push against the wind.

post break-up reflections from the house that I still lived in after she left

Once Our Shoes Are Off

I guess I want to be your ride home.
Not because you owe it to me,
or I want to be above you,
but because that's where you're going.
I'd like to be there too.

I'd like to wrap my arms about you,
your's as much 'round me,
to kiss you once our shoes are off,
to place them by the door.

I know that you've got things to do
and tomorrow's just as busy,
but for just tonight could we brush our teeth,
could we stay up late to talk?

I'd like to see the ceiling move,
to rumble toward the stairs.
That's us, you know:
bright lights burning up.
I'd like to spend some time with you.

It's all I've got, time and patience;
I'll give you that
and the other I'd share with you freely.

I wanted to play house with someone so bad

Sometimes The Clouds

Sometimes the clouds
have to fall
before the sun's seen shining.
It is, although, there all the while
as bright as before and it's patient.

Then let us aim toward the end of the tunnel,
arriving about mid-October,
and from then be consumed
by that which we're creating, or indulge,
indeed, in the thing which we've made

Only space and time stand between us,
and a kiss just made it in moments.
All I need is a bus.

from gathered mushy texts, combined to make a poem

We Had Moments

fairly
and accurate
we were some
thing else
entirely,
still,
we had moments
we made contact with
hearts, drew them out, shook
them up and for that,
I would do it
all over
again.

Broke With Flesh

I broke with flesh to speak with you freely.
I do not flatter.
I've not held up highly before,
and this does not need wrists, but rests.

I can't explain it, but I welcome it
with open arms and eager heart.
Sometimes you can't push,
but you can never anticipate falling.
I'd fall into this.

Bodies don't need to be so consequential
as they've been before and besides,
we knew silently before parting.

sappy texts turned into a poem #741

The Story, Old

I had higher hopes for this tree root cathedral.
Her crowns were cast in bronze and dreams,
bejeweled by glitter and
set aside.

There was little about
and the story,
old.
By the time my tummy settled,
by the day I took her there, there
was little left to do but wander.

When we breathed,
it was more like snowflakes:

She was pretty but she'd never last.
She'd seen no wonder and that would not do.

translation: dating her was just okay

Love Need Not Be

I think that love need
not be rare, nor special, unique
or in any way unheard of -
it need only be precious
for there's precious little left
and so many souls are left sorely in need.

I think that love might
need introduction - love,
this is Someone,
someone, a Friend.

friend, this is someone who probably won't call you back

There When I Do

I am curled up in blankets and sheets,
swimming in pillow cases,
naked, drunk with laughter.

For as much as you are not here with me now,
you are under these covers
and arms wrapped around me.
I hold you as tight as eyes locked two to other.
Your lips are pressed and fingers tracing jawline,
contours, neck and ears,
one hand by the small of your back.

I kiss you good night and fall to sleep
with violet hair tickling my cheeks.
I am lucky and dream.
You are there when I do.

By the coast and the sky
and the breeze filling shirts up,
our eyes are both closed.
Our fingers are too,
but to mine wrapped with yours in,
to yours filled with mine.

this may be the most roundabout way to ask to spoon with me ever

My Rainbow Shoes

"The wind," I say,
but it weren't no stiff breeze that brought me here.
It was a thousand lazy roundabouts,
and whether within or without the confines of
means or reason, it was something there
that set about fat feet to pounding pavement.
Strong hands were gripping guard rails
while my eyes were warm and glazed,
and of all the self-righteous glances mincing words
with soft teeth and forked tongue,
how many are written by the pen hand of a free-man?
How many by a second-rate poet?

Clear your throat. Clear your mind.

So… my rainbow shoes did dances,
high step and tip-toed along the border.
No socks to warm the trough and peak,
and gaps to meet the day by way of stone and grass.
See, my mind is lent to bend and twist,
taps and spirals set to tunes of sweltering ecstasy.
Here by the aching stomach of this river,
I have found some common ground to land on,
where harsh words and humble bones
hide behind the sagging swagger of eyes closed
and lips uplifted, and you ask what brings me to town.

"The wind," I say,
but it weren't no stiff breeze that brought me here.
The air was taut and humid, pressure rising,
eyes intensify, my skin grew cold and clammy,
hair raising, flared nostrils,
beady black pupil holding tight to sky blue iris,
but wait! That girl is crazy.

My rainbow shoes were glued to ground,
although my feet were hardly steady;
and my back and forehead were shining sweaty,
but there was no one to call my own.
Sure there were some faces,
a couple of bodies and a soul or two,
but no one to call my own.

I mean, I had a door, a lock, a key, a bed,
a car, a job, a phone, a head
         (though, a head consumed of a mind by brain
         still stuck to the hip of the leg of the girl who was gone)

I took to the streets.

My legs were rubber bands stretched wet
in the heat of the high of the here and now,
Blankets wrapped all their beautiful bodies;
days were hot and nights were lonesome.
By the side of the girl who was nervous to meet me,
I spoke of my life and love lost.
Dinner was wonderful that night –
the guts of a compost bin,
vegan with greens we picked in the Golden Gate.

But, like any dumb, downtrodden dog,
I came back home with less than I left with.
I beat myself as I have no master,
no one to tell me how wrong I've been,
and no one to call my own,
and you ask what brings me here.

"The wind," I say,
for the winds of change can barrel over
all of the high and haughty notions
we clutch close to our breasts.
The wind, both destructive and lovely,
pushed past the bared and frozen bones,
eating into the meat of it,
feathers lifting into wings of golden glory,
hazy hues of soft and silent subtle motion.
The winds of change tore my roots from soil,
but my wings did lift and lay me down,
here in the aching, sobbing breast of this river

"Welcome home," she seems to say. *"Welcome home."*

my first slam poem, circa 25 years

Weeks, Each Waning, Pale

They're not just words,
they're two hearts melding, separated
only by the backyard
which is our playground.

I am on my way and these weeks,
each waning, pale
when held to the coming months
and, if my tummy speaks truly,
for our fingers to touch and tingle.

If I have your fingers,
heart and song to look forward to,
then I could wait just as long as I have to.
Paired hearts can perfect patience.

Goddamn These Fingers

Some time we had there -
        are you also coming with us?
              we'll tear our limbs like
                      leaves from trees or
                      paint from fences
and walk the
        streets with
              smiles widened -
              are you also pulling with us?
The weight's
              not more
but goddamn   than one strong back's worth
        these fingers
              are slip
pin
g

you're either with us, or you're against us, or something else entirely

Fistful Of Wet Matches

Most fires only last half the night,
but my fingers have lit fuses
that burned and still burn,
and with only a fistful of wet matches,
that's right, and with no tinder,
and in the rain no less,
and when the matches wouldn't strike
I borrowed a lighter,
and since I had no shelter,
I borrowed that too,
and when the fuse was lit and wanting
I walked away
and I left them to it
because I was in a borrowed home
with only a fist of wet matches,
and the night was halfway through.

it's not a humble brag if you made it up

Totally Not About Weed Club

The first rule of Weed Club is: always talk about Weed Club.
The second rule of Weed Club is: always – no, wait,
       NEVER – talk about... umm, hold on. Okay,
The second rule of Weed Club is: no rules, man.

Yeah. Blows your mind, right?

Yeah, cause I'm an activist, like,
this is what I do, this is the real shit.
Okay, like – wait, it was this rope company,
and like, a paint company too, it's like,
the emperor wears no clothes.

Think about it.
Who took his clothes?

Yeah. Blows your mind, right?

wait, what were we talking about?

Day Begins Anew

This is the beginning.
This is the end.
Nothing else can ever come from this,
   nothing good,
   nothing bad.
This is where the rubber
meets the road
my shoes
meet the sidewalk,
the day begins anew.

This is for me. This is for you.
I've got two worn out pictures
   both aged and withered eyes
   but the precipice we stand to
is revealing sea and sky
   the land falls out before us
   so close we cannot see.

This here's for you, my darling.
This here's for you and me.

hyperbole is literally the worst thing in the entire world

Consolation Tacos

He's still something else and I've walked off the boarding.
My eyes brim with laughter, my throat seize in pain
and the day into streetlight in some nowhere Nor-Cal,
in a house we were paid to leave from
when there was nowhere else to go.

I wondered where you were and my boots beat the concrete,
blocks of frustrated and fruitless delay.

Panic, relax, find your center,
he's nowhere, he's gone, relax,
center- panic! He's gone.
Cue the sound effects-
a cold wind.

Go back, trace your footsteps,
cry on a park bench.
I'm so goddamn hungry.
Forty-nine cent burritos,
red + green sauce and
settle out details.
Calm my stomach.
Center.

Call the cops-
they haven't seen him either.
Why the fuck did I call the cops?

I found him on a table, laid back and breathing smoke.
Where ya been, he asked.
I got some cash and free sandwich, you hungry?

I told him I'd already eaten.

there is nothing bad that the cops can't make worse

Your Things Today

I went through your things today
and found mementos from your old life.
I read pain and coughing, crows
from throat that held back-

I went through your things today
and found the reason why I found you,
why you were out there in the first place,
so you could ask me for a lighter.

Having gone through your things,
I am seeing light as told me
without boom or thunderclap,
no shout, congratulations.

A call to home connects to you
and words do change as minds do too.
I am draped by that which I wanted to warm with,
that blanket poured over our heads.

Now that we're down here
and curled up in bedsheets,
there's no more right future than
here with you nightly
and there with you daytime.

I went through your things today
and found omens of past,
not a gift or the present,
but of night's dawning shadow.

The sun is now up.

I went through your things
and I put them each back.
Those crows coughed up and their talons away -

now there's no need for fear and I'm ready for you.

Your things that I went through today
were handed to me,
four lines on a page
never written for me,
so I hand them all back
or to sides or within me.
I trust that I'll see them again.

note: snooping through people's things is rude

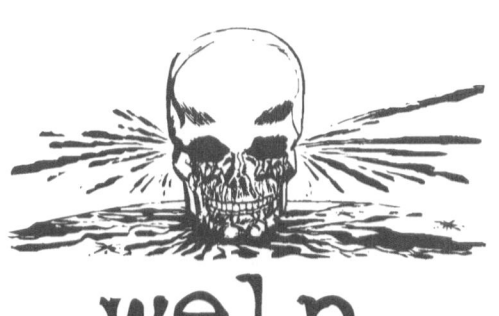

welp.

willowpaloma@riseup.net

All poems written by Willow P. Woolf, no rights reserved
Formatted using elementary OS, LibreOffice 6.0 and GIMP 2.8
Fonts: My Underwood, Free Serif, Pirates Two, Horror Dingbats,
Front cover design background is Letter P from Horror Dingbats
Back cover design background is Letter L from Vieraskirjan Peto

www.ingramcontent.com/pod-product-compliance
Lightning Source LLC
Chambersburg PA
CBHW030902180526
45163CB00004B/1663